UNDERSTANDING FRACTIONS
COLOURING WORKBOOK

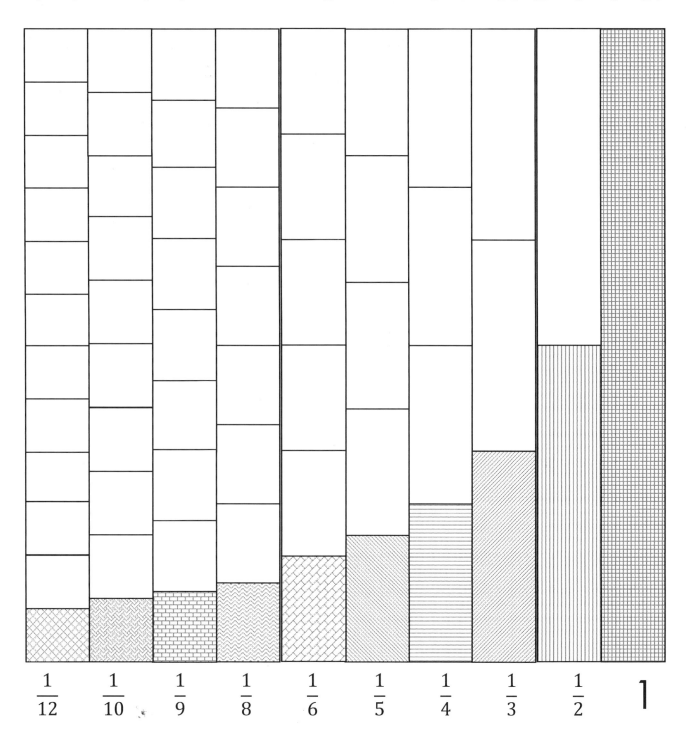

ENG S JAMA

author.to/FractionsVisually

Copyright © Eng S Jama
All rights reserved
FractionsVisually.com

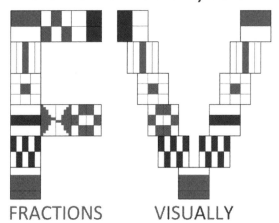
FRACTIONS   VISUALLY

Thank you for buying my book and helping the author to keep on writing. ☺

I hope you'll enjoy reading UNDERSTANDING FRACTIONS VISUALLY: COLOURING WORKBOOK.

If so, please, consider leaving a review on **Amazon.com** @ amazon.com/review/create-review?&asin=**1723563986**. A single line, short sentence, few phrases or just rating will do.

If not, please, send me your feedback, comments and corrections to: eng-s-jama@fractionsvisually.com.

Thanks.

--- *Series #2:* ADDING FRACTIONS VISUALLY ---

Colouring workbook: mybook.to/WB2-Sh   **Paperback**: mybook.to/B-2
Colour paperback: mybook.to/B2-C   **Colour ebook**: mybook.to/eB2-C
Workbook: mybook.to/WB2   **Colour workbook**: mybook.to/WB2-C

--- *Series #3:* ADDING FRACTIONS STEP-BY-STEP ---

Paperback: mybook.to/B-3   **Colour paperback**: mybook.to/B3-C
Workbook: mybook.to/WB3   **Colour workbook**: mybook.to/WB3-C

--- *Series #4:* UNDERSTAND, ADD & SUBTRACT FRACTIONS VISUALLY ---

Paperback: mybook.to/B-4   **Colour paperback**: mybook.to/B4-C

UNDERSTANDING FRACTIONS VISUALLY
COLOURING WORKBOOK

Ages 5-11, **Grades** K-5th grade and **Years** 1-6

Maths fractions made fun and visual

For visual learner children who find text-based fractions no fun

Colouring, shading, tracing ...

The fastest way to learn fractions, very easily!

Have fun!

Also available

Colouring **workbook**: mybook.to/WB1-Sh-v2   **Paperback**: mybook.to/B-1

Colour **paperback**: mybook.to/B1-C   **Colour ebook**: mybook.to/eB1-C

Workbook: mybook.to/WB-1   Colour **workbook**: mybook.to/WB1-C

Free e-Book

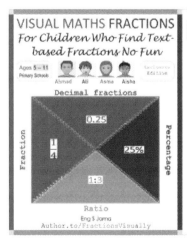

MASTER MATHS FRACTIONS VISUALLY
FOR VISUAL LEARNER CHILDREN AND
ADULTS WHO ARE STILL SCARED OF FRACTIONS

HATE FRACTIONS?
VISUAL MATHS FRACTIONS will change all that!
*It is completely **Free** - nothing to lose to try it.*
This visual e-book will surprise you how easy it is
to master maths fractions. **Download** it NOW!

Signup for my **FREE** e-book & exclusive content @ FractionsVisually.com

Contents

Page(s)

Fractions Chart 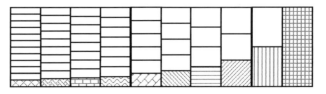 i

Halving 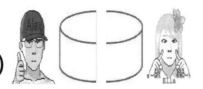 4 – 23
(Sharing equally for 2 people)

Introduction to Fractions 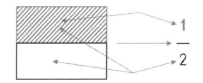 24

Thirds 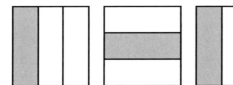 25 – 27

Quartering  28 – 47
(Sharing equally for 4 people)

Equivalent Fractions  48 – 50

Fifths 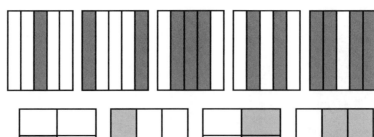 51 – 55

Sixths 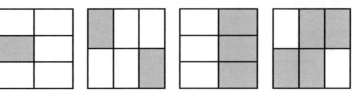 56 – 64

Contents   Page(s)

Eighths   65 – 75

Quiz 1   76

Ninths   77 – 87

Tenths   88 – 102

Quiz 2   103

$\frac{1}{2}$ $\frac{1}{3}$ $\frac{1}{5}$ $\frac{1}{4}$ $\frac{1}{6}$ $\frac{1}{9}$

$\frac{1}{7}$ $\frac{3}{4}$ $\frac{1}{8}$ $\frac{1}{10}$ $\frac{1}{1}$ 1

Copyright & Series Titles   104

Book Description   105

Halving 2

Alex and **Ella** are friends and often share things _equally_.

Colour and trace the following **shape** for **Alex** and **Ella** _fairly_.

*Some **examples** are partially **done** for you.* Good Luck!

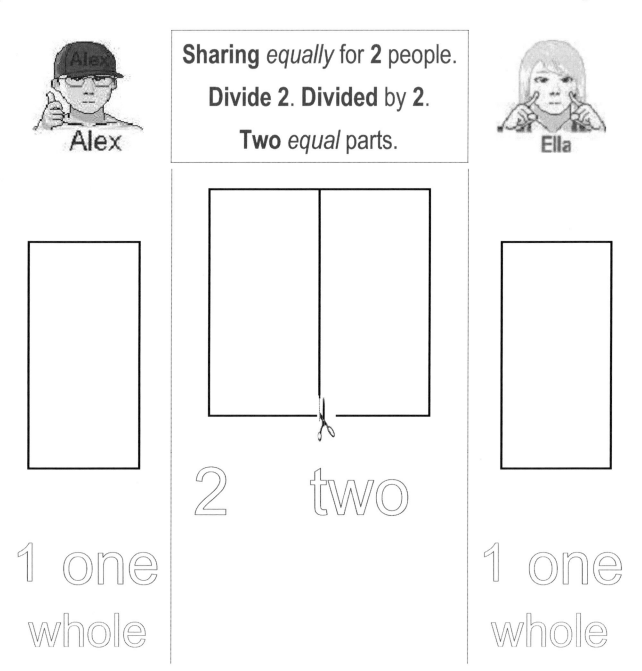

Halving 4

Colour and **shade** the following shape for **Alex** and **Ella** _equally._
Use your imagination how to colour, **shade** and trace!

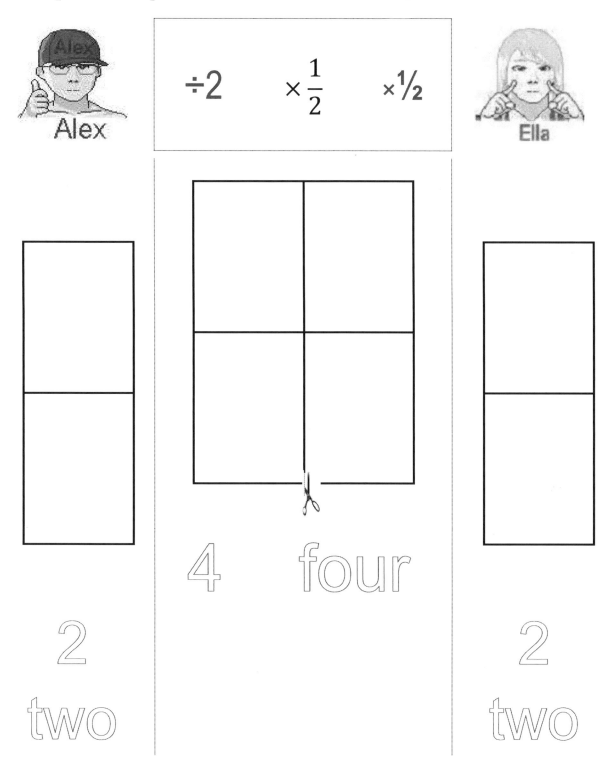

Halving 6

Colour and **shade** the following shape for **Alex** and **Ella** *fairly.*

Use your imagination how to colour, **shade** and trace!

Sharing *equally* for **2** people.

Divide 2. **Divided** by **2**.

Two *equal* parts.

Alex

Ella

6 six

3 3

three three

Halving 8

Colour and **shade** the following shape for **Alex** and **Ella** *equally.*
Use your imagination how to colour, **shade** and trace!

÷2   × $\frac{1}{2}$ × $^1\!/_2$

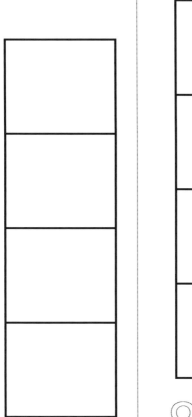
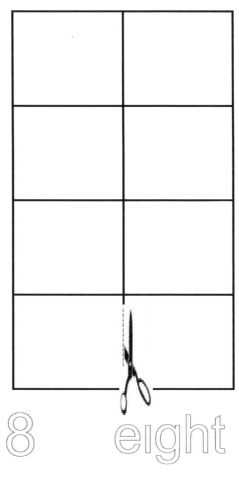

8 eight

4   4
four four

Halving 10

Colour and **shade** the following shape for **Alex** and **Ella** _fairly._
Use your imagination how to colour, **shade** and trace!

Alex

Sharing _equally_ for **2** people.
Divide 2. **Divided** by **2**.
Two _equal_ parts.

Ella

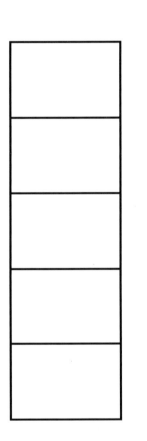
5
five

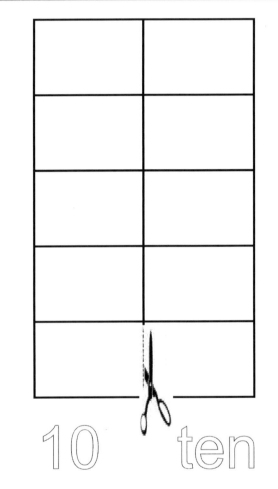
10   ten

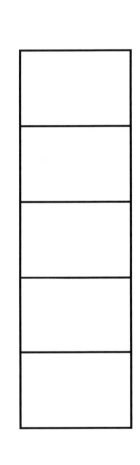
5
five

Halving 12

Colour and **shade** the following shape for **Alex** and **Ella** *equally.*
Use your imagination how to colour, **shade** and trace!

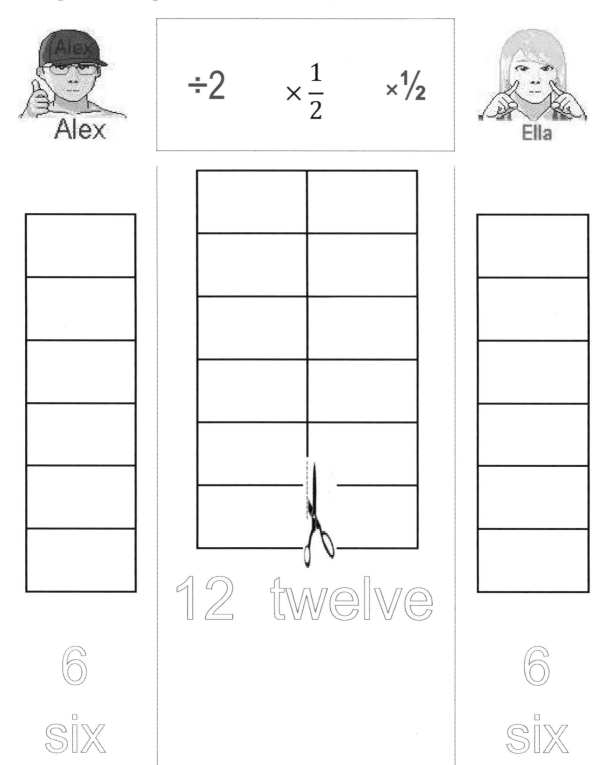

Halving 14

Colour and **shade** the following shape for **Alex** and **Ella** *fairly.*
Use your imagination how to colour, **shade** and trace!

Sharing *equally* for **2** people.
Divide 2. **Divided** by **2**.
Two *equal* parts.

Alex

Ella

14 fourteen

7
seven

7
seven

Halving 16

Colour and **shade** the following shape for **Alex** and **Ella** _equally._
Use your imagination how to colour, **shade** and trace!

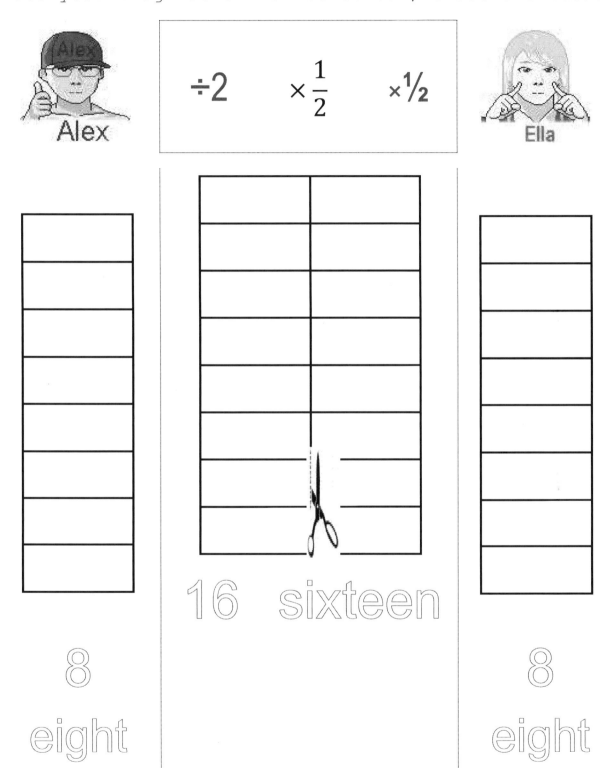

Halving 18

Colour and **shade** the following shape for **Alex** and **Ella** *fairly.*
Use your imagination how to colour, **shade** and trace!

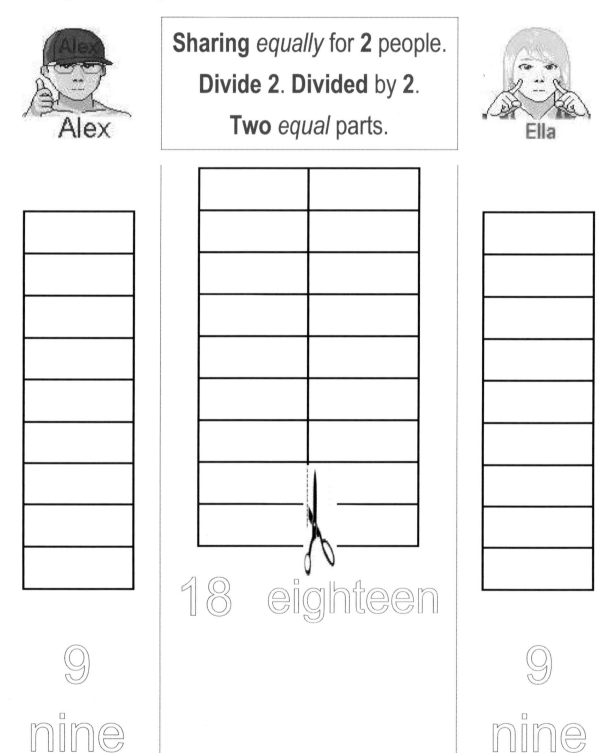

Halving 20

Colour and **shade** the following shape for **Alex** and **Ella** *equally.*
Use your imagination how to colour, **shade** and trace!

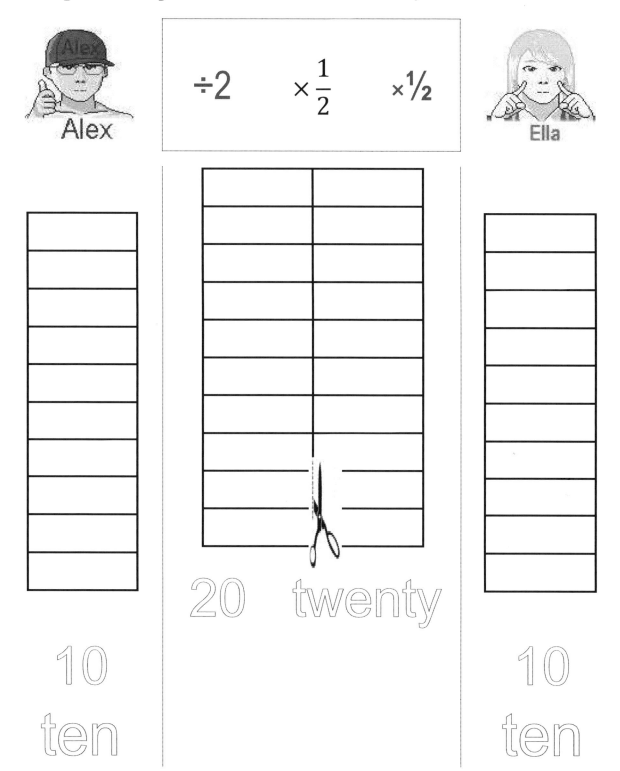

Halving 1

Colour and **shade** the following shape for **Alex** and **Ella** *fairly.*
Use your imagination how to colour, **shade** and trace!

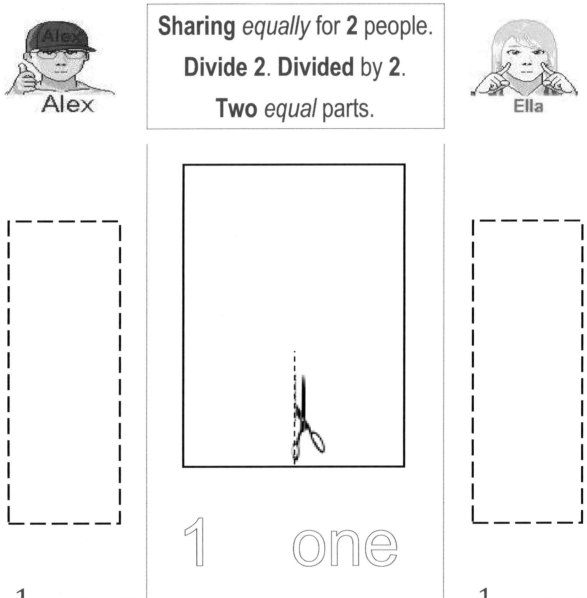

Halving 3

Colour and **shade** the following shape for **Alex** and **Ella** *equally.*
Use your imagination how to colour, **shade** and trace!

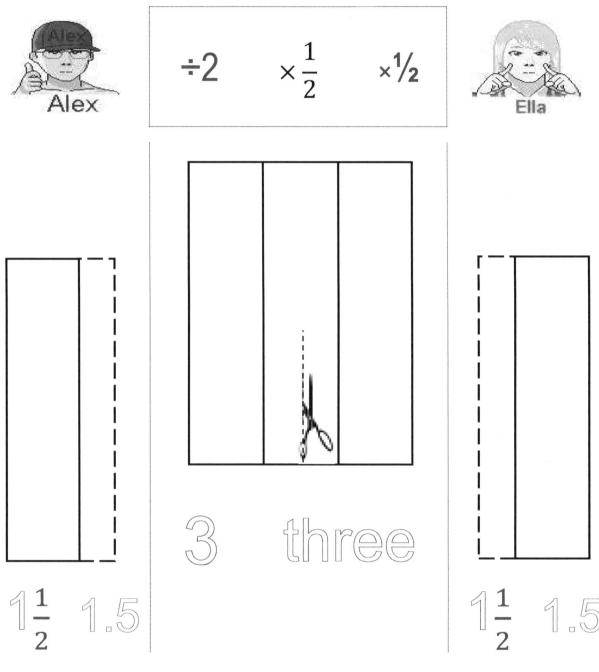

Halving 5

Colour and **shade** the following shape for **Alex** and **Ella** *fairly.*
Use your imagination how to colour, **shade** and trace!

Sharing *equally* for **2** people.
Divide 2. **Divided** by **2**.
Two *equal* parts.

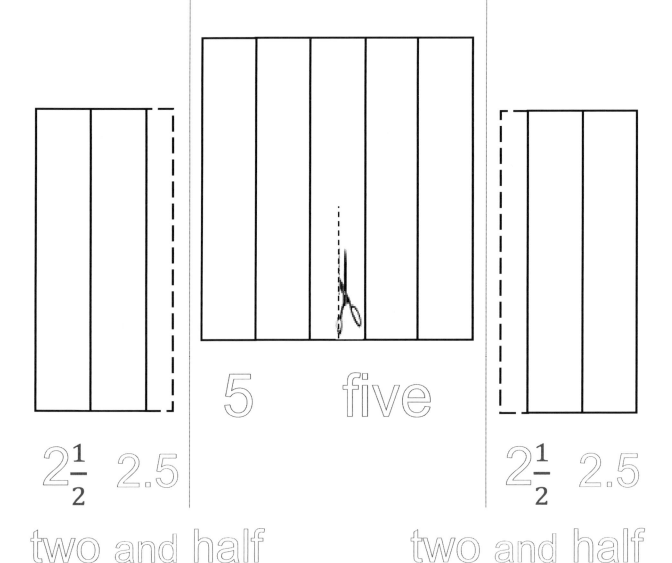

Halving 7

Colour and **shade** the following shape for **Alex** and **Ella** *equally.*
Use your imagination how to colour, **shade** and trace!

$$\div 2 \qquad \times \frac{1}{2} \qquad \times \tfrac{1}{2}$$

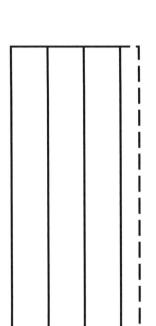
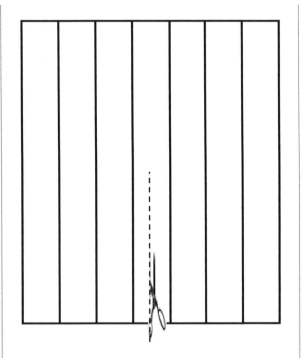
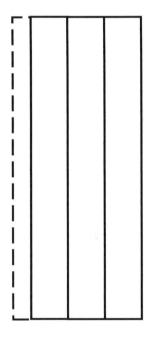

7 seven

$3\tfrac{1}{2}$ 3.5 $3\tfrac{1}{2}$ 3.5

three and half   three and half

Halving 9

Colour and **shade** the following shape for **Alex** and **Ella** *fairly.*
Use your imagination how to colour, **shade** and trace!

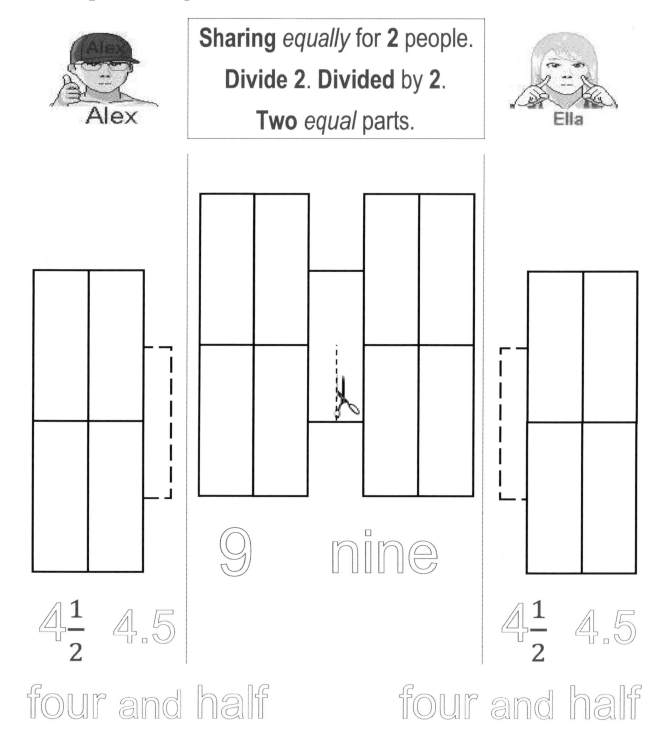

Halving 11

Colour and **shade** the following shape for **Alex** and **Ella** *equally.*
Use your imagination how to colour, **shade** and trace!

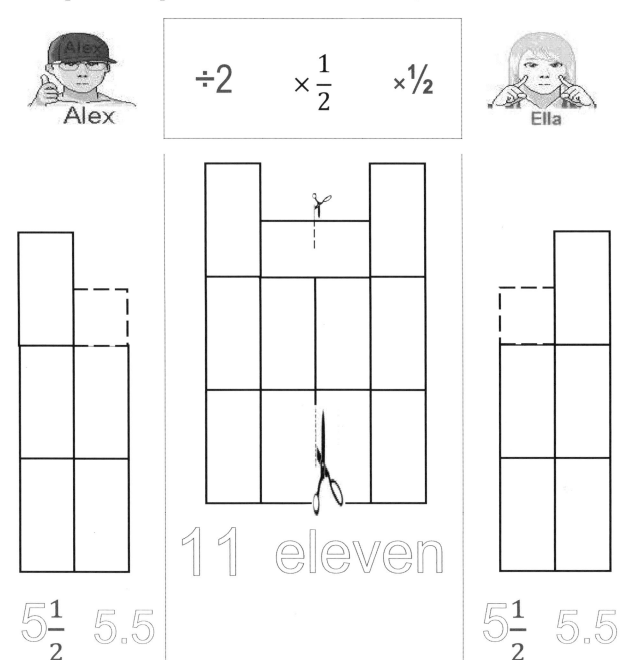

Halving 13

Colour and **shade** the following shape for **Alex** and **Ella** _fairly._

Use your imagination how to colour, **shade** and trace!

Sharing _equally_ for **2** people.
Divide 2. **Divided** by **2**.
Two _equal_ parts.

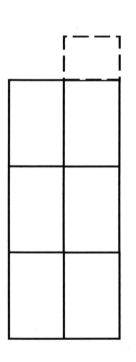

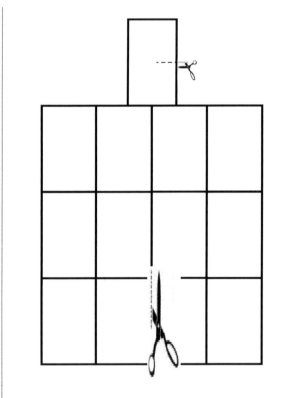

13 thirteen

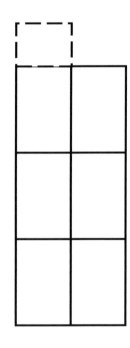

$6\frac{1}{2}$ 6.5

six and half

$6\frac{1}{2}$ 6.5

six and half

Halving 15

Colour and **shade** the following shape for **Alex** and **Ella** *equally*.

Use your imagination how to colour, **shade** and trace!

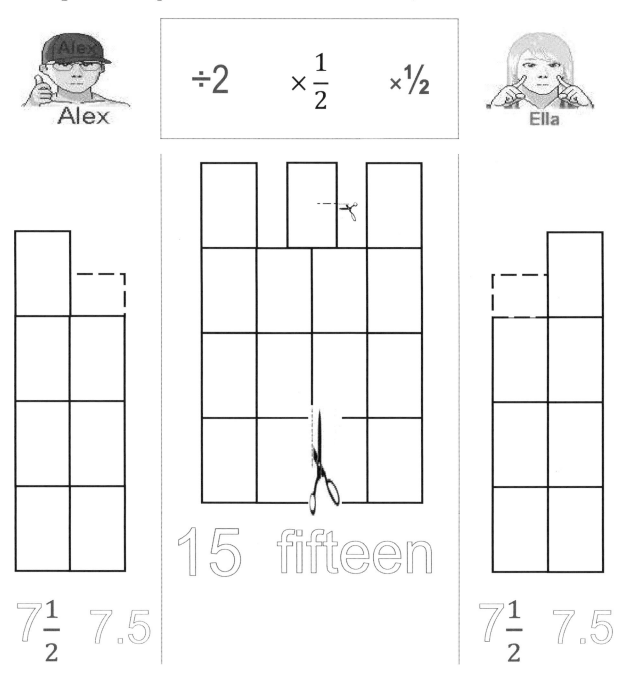

Halving 17

Colour and **shade** the following shape for **Alex** and **Ella** *fairly.*
Use your imagination how to colour, **shade** and trace!

Sharing *equally* for **2** people.
Divide 2. Divided by **2**.
Two *equal* parts.

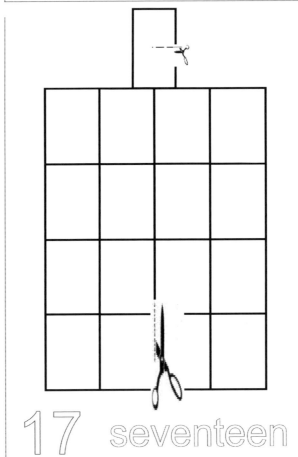

17 seventeen

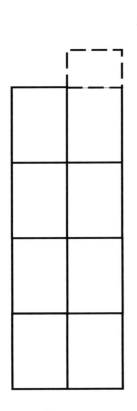

8 1/2   8.5

eight and half

8 1/2   8.5

eight and half

Halving 19

Colour and **shade** the following shape for **Alex** and **Ella** *equally.*
Use your imagination how to colour, **shade** and trace!

÷2   × $\frac{1}{2}$ × ½

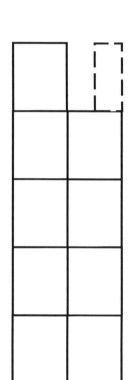
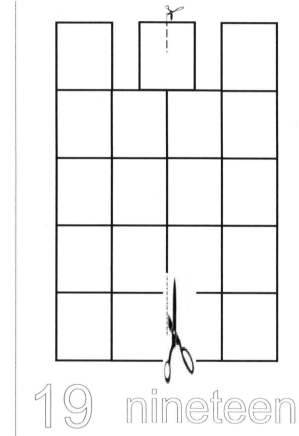
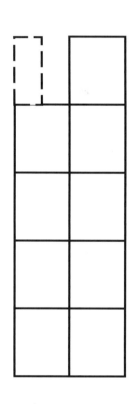

19 nineteen

$9\frac{1}{2}$ 9.5

nine and half

$9\frac{1}{2}$ 9.5

nine and half

23

What is a fraction?

Fraction is a **part** or **parts** of a **whole**.

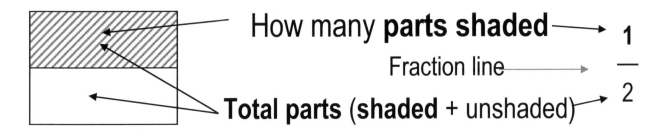

- **Top** number (*numerator*) shows **how many** parts (out of a whole)
- **Bottom** number (*denominator*) means **total** parts (to make whole)

One part is **shaded** out of **two** parts. That is a **half** or **one-half**. $\frac{1}{2}$

Also, **one** part is unshaded out of **two** parts. That is another **half** or **one-half**. $\frac{1}{2}$

And $\frac{1}{2}$ + $\frac{1}{2}$ = $\frac{2}{2}$ = 1

A **fraction** can be:

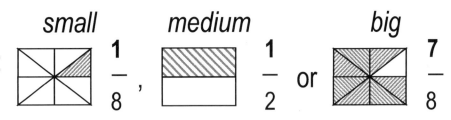

small $\frac{1}{8}$, medium $\frac{1}{2}$ or big $\frac{7}{8}$

---

*But **not** as **big** as a **whole** like* 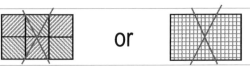 or

- A proper **fraction** is <u>always</u> *smaller* or *less* than a **whole**!

Thirds of 3

Sharing *equally* for **3** people. Divided by 3. Three equal parts…

÷3	× $\frac{1}{3}$	× $^1/_3$

Use your imagination how to colour, **shade** and trace.

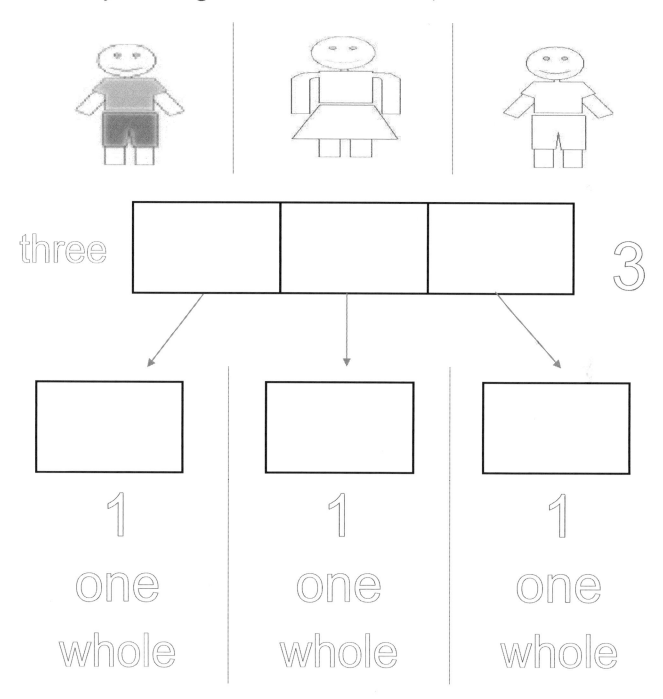

Thirds of 1

Sharing *equally* for **3** people. Divided by 3. Three equal parts…

÷3	× $\frac{1}{3}$	× $^1/_3$

Use your imagination how to colour, **shade** and trace.

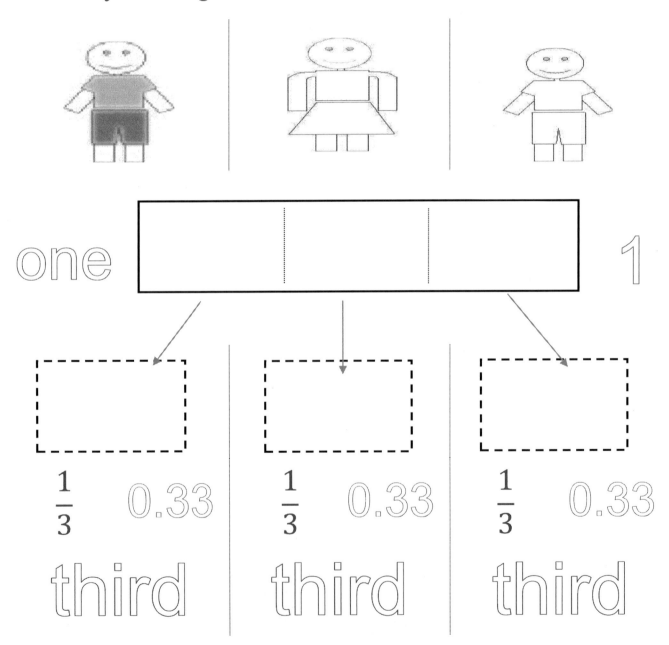

Thirds of 2

Sharing *equally* for **3** people. Divided by 3. Three equal parts...

| ÷3 | × 1/3 | × ¹⁄₃ |

Use your imagination how to colour, **shade** and trace.

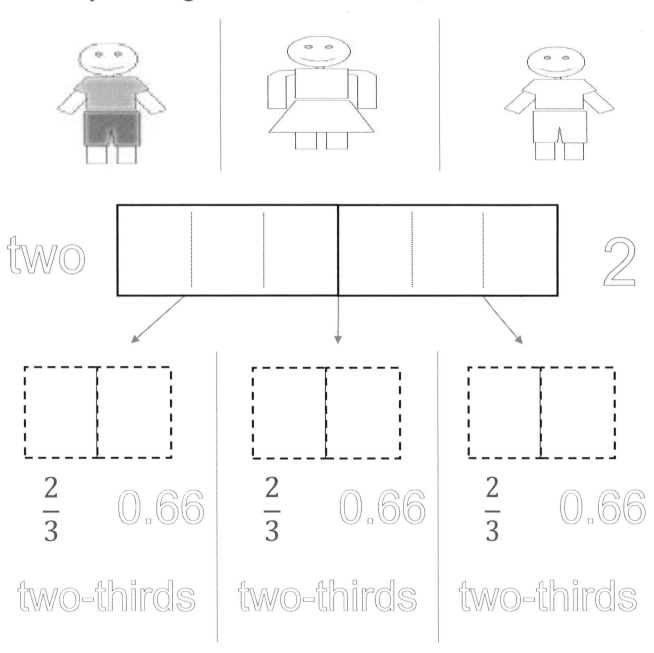

two　　　　　　　　　　　　　　　　2

2/3　0.66　　　2/3　0.66　　　2/3　0.66

two-thirds　　two-thirds　　two-thirds

Quartering 4

Alex and **Ella** also share things with their friends **Ali** and **Asha**.

For the following shapes, everyone gets a **quarter** (one-fourth) or **half** of **half**! That's **halving** for two groups. Then **halving** *again* for each.

Use your imagination how to colour, **shade** and trace!

Sharing *equally* for **4** people.
Divided by 4. Four equal parts

$÷4 \qquad ×\frac{1}{4} \qquad ×¼$

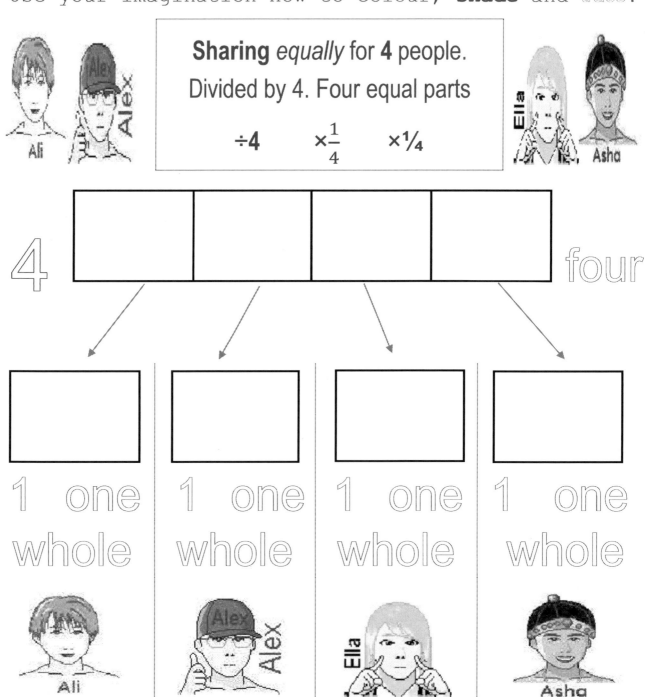

Quartering 8

Use your imagination how to colour, **shade** and trace!

Sharing *equally* for **4** people.
Divide 4. **Four** *equal* parts. **Divided** by 4.

$\div 4$ $\times \frac{1}{4}$ $\times \frac{1}{4}$

8

eight

2 two

2 two

2 two

2 two

Quartering 12

Use your imagination how to colour, **shade** and trace!

Sharing *equally* for **4** people. **Divide** 4. **Four** *equal* parts. **Divided** by 4
÷4   ×$\frac{1}{4}$ ×¼

12

twelve

3 three

3 three

3 three

3 three

Quartering 16

Use your imagination how to colour, **shade** and trace!

Sharing *equally* for **4** people.
Divide 4. **Four** *equal* parts. **Divided** by 4

÷4   ×$\frac{1}{4}$ ×¼

16

4 four

4 four

4 four

4 four

sixteen

Quartering 20

Use your imagination how to colour, **shade** and trace!

> **Sharing** *equally* for **4** people.
> **Divide** 4. **Four** *equal* parts. **Divided** by 4
> ÷4   ×$\frac{1}{4}$ ×¼

20

5 five

5 five

5 five

5 five

twenty

Quartering 2

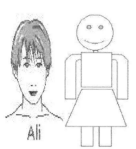

Sharing *equally* for **4** people.
Divided by 4. Four equal parts

÷4   ×$\frac{1}{4}$ ×¼

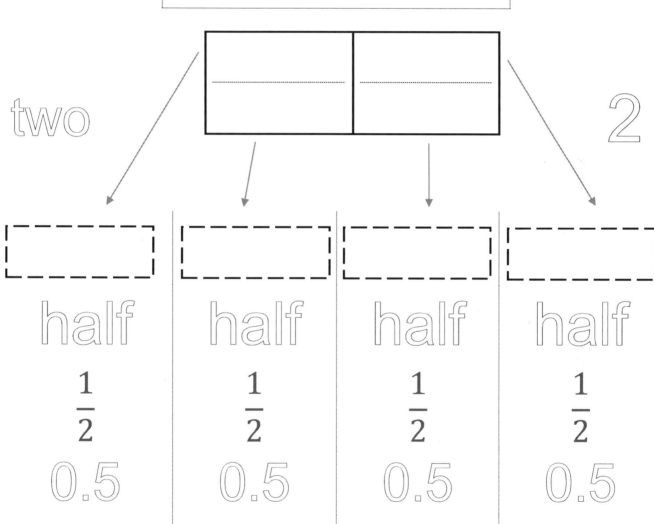

two

2

half   half   half   half

$\frac{1}{2}$ $\frac{1}{2}$ $\frac{1}{2}$ $\frac{1}{2}$

0.5   0.5   0.5   0.5

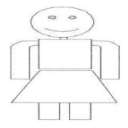

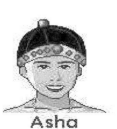

Quartering 6

Use your imagination how to colour, **shade** and trace!

Sharing *equally* for **4** people.
Divide 4. **Four** *equal* parts. **Divided** by **4**

÷4   ×$\frac{1}{4}$ ×¼

six 6

Ali Ella Asha

one and a half | one and a half | one and a half | one and a half

$1\frac{1}{2}$ 1.5 | $1\frac{1}{2}$ 1.5 | $1\frac{1}{2}$ 1.5 | $1\frac{1}{2}$ 1.5

Quartering 10

Use your imagination how to colour, **shade** and trace!

Sharing *equally* for **4** people.
Divide 4. **Four** *equal* parts. **Divided** by **4**

$÷4$ $×\dfrac{1}{4}$ $×¼$

ten   10

Ali   Ella   Asha

two and a half | two and a half | two and a half | two and a half

$2\dfrac{1}{2}$ 2.5 | $2\dfrac{1}{2}$ 2.5 | $2\dfrac{1}{2}$ 2.5 | $2\dfrac{1}{2}$ 2.5

Quartering 14

Use your imagination how to colour, **shade** and trace!

Sharing *equally* for **4** people.
Divide 4. **Four** *equal* parts. **Divided** by **4**

÷4   ×$\frac{1}{4}$ ×¼

four-teen   14

Ali   Ella   Asha

three and half | three and half | three and half | three and half

$3\frac{1}{2}$ 3.5 | $3\frac{1}{2}$ 3.5 | $3\frac{1}{2}$ 3.5 | $3\frac{1}{2}$ 3.5

Quartering 18

Use your imagination how to colour, **shade** and trace!

Sharing *equally* for **4** people.
Divide 4. **Four** *equal* parts. **Divided** by **4**

÷4   ×$\frac{1}{4}$ ×¼

eigh-teen   18

Ali   Ella   Asha

four and a half | four and a half | four and a half | four and a half

$4\frac{1}{2}$ 4.50 | $4\frac{1}{2}$ 4.50 | $4\frac{1}{2}$ 4.50 | $4\frac{1}{2}$ 4.50

Quartering 1

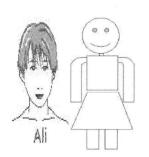
Ali

Sharing *equally* for **4** people.
Divided by 4. Four equal parts

$\div 4$ $\times \frac{1}{4}$ $\times \frac{1}{4}$

Ella   Asha

one

1

quarter | quarter | quarter | quarter

$\frac{1}{4}$ | $\frac{1}{4}$ | $\frac{1}{4}$ | $\frac{1}{4}$

0.25 | 0.25 | 0.25 | 0.25

 Ali | 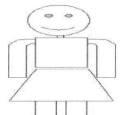 |  Ella | 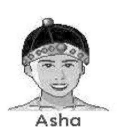 Asha

38

Quartering 5

Use your imagination how to colour, **shade** and trace!

Sharing *equally* for **4** people.
Divide 4. **Four** *equal* parts. **Divided** by **4**

$\div 4$ $\times \frac{1}{4}$ $\times ¼$

five   5

Ali   Ella   Asha

one and a quarter | one and a quarter | one and a quarter | one and a quarter

$1\frac{1}{4}$ 1.25 | $1\frac{1}{4}$ 1.25 | $1\frac{1}{4}$ 1.25 | $1\frac{1}{4}$ 1.25

Quartering 9

Use your imagination how to colour, **shade** and trace!

> **Sharing** *equally* for **4** people.
> **Divide** 4. **Four** *equal* parts. **Divided** by **4**
> ÷4   ×$\frac{1}{4}$ ×¼

nine   9

Ali   Ella   Asha

two and a quarter | two and a quarter | two and a quarter | two and quarter

$2\frac{1}{4}$ 2.25 | $2\frac{1}{4}$ 2.25 | $2\frac{1}{4}$ 2.25 | $2\frac{1}{4}$ 2.25

Quartering 13

Use your imagination how to colour, **shade** and trace!

Sharing *equally* for **4** people.
Divide 4. **Four** *equal* parts. **Divided** by **4**

÷4   ×$\frac{1}{4}$ ×¼

thir-
teen   13

Ali   Ella   Asha

three and | three and | three and | three and
a quarter | a quarter | a quarter | a quarter

$3\frac{1}{4}$ 3.25 $3\frac{1}{4}$ 3.25 $3\frac{1}{4}$ 3.25 $3\frac{1}{4}$ 3.25

Quartering 17

Use your *imagination* how to colour, **shade** and trace!

Sharing *equally* for **4** people.
Divide 4. **Four** *equal* parts. **Divided** by **4**

÷4   ×$\frac{1}{4}$ ×¼

seven-
teen

17

Ali   Ella   Asha

| four and a quarter | four and a quarter | four and a quarter | four and a quarter |

$4\frac{1}{4}$ 4.25 | $4\frac{1}{4}$ 4.25 | $4\frac{1}{4}$ 4.25 | $4\frac{1}{4}$ 4.25

Quartering 3

Sharing *equally* for **4** people.
Divided by 4. Four equal parts

÷**4**   ×$\frac{1}{4}$ ×¼

three   3

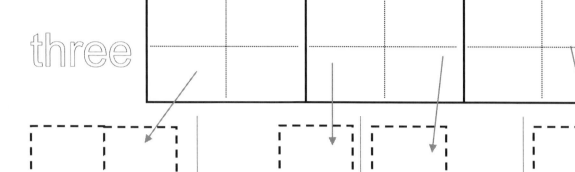

three-quarters   three-quarters   three-quarters   three-quarters

$\frac{3}{4}$ $\frac{3}{4}$ $\frac{3}{4}$ $\frac{3}{4}$

0.75   0.75   0.75   0.75

 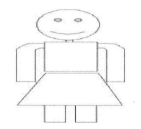  

Quartering 7

Ali

Sharing *equally* for **4** people.
Divided by 4. Four equal parts

÷4   ×$\frac{1}{4}$ ×¼

Ella Asha

seven   7

one and three-quarters | one and three-quarters | one and three-quarters | one and three-quarters
$1\frac{3}{4}$ | $1\frac{3}{4}$ | $1\frac{3}{4}$ | $1\frac{3}{4}$
1.75 | 1.75 | 1.75 | 1.75

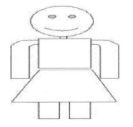

44

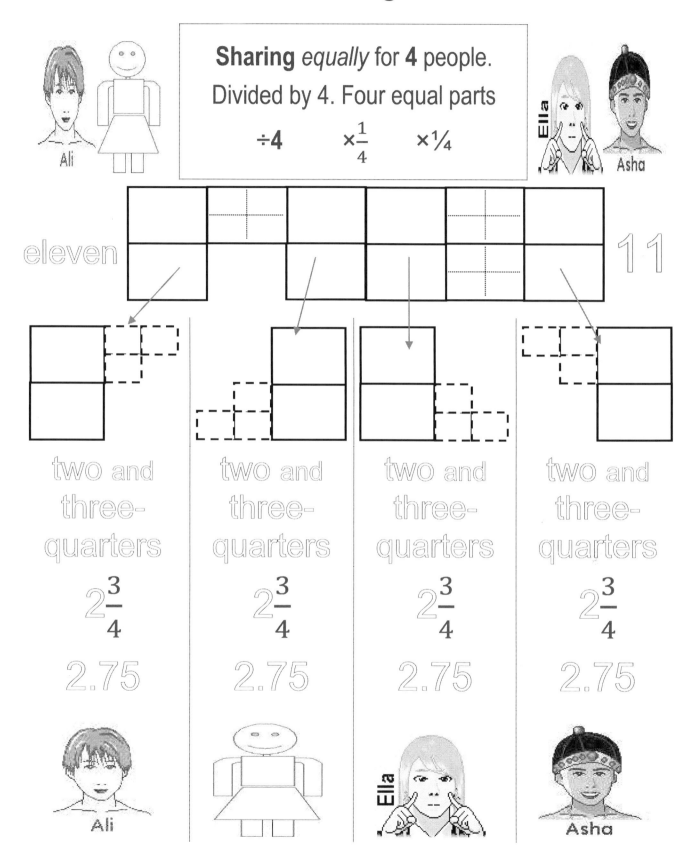

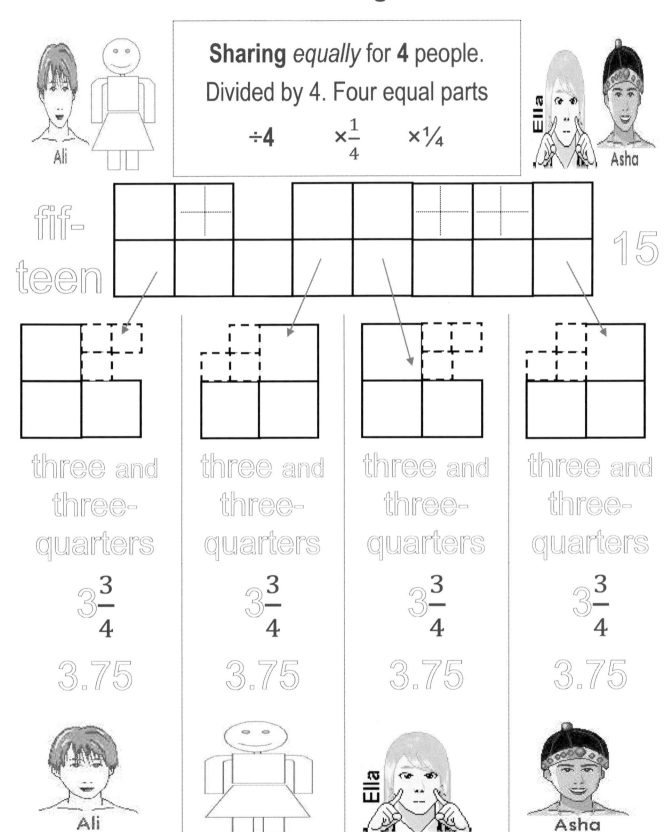

Quartering 19

Sharing *equally* for **4** people.
Divided by 4. Four equal parts

÷4   ×$\frac{1}{4}$ ×¼

nine-
teen

19

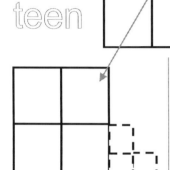

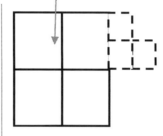

four and three-quarters

$4\frac{3}{4}$

4.75

four and three-quarters

$4\frac{3}{4}$

4.75

four and three-quarters

$4\frac{3}{4}$

4.75

four and three-quarters

$4\frac{3}{4}$

4.75

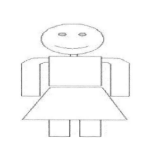

Equivalent Fractions

Equivalent means *equal in value*.

For example, if **2** children share **1** whole cake, they each get a **half**.

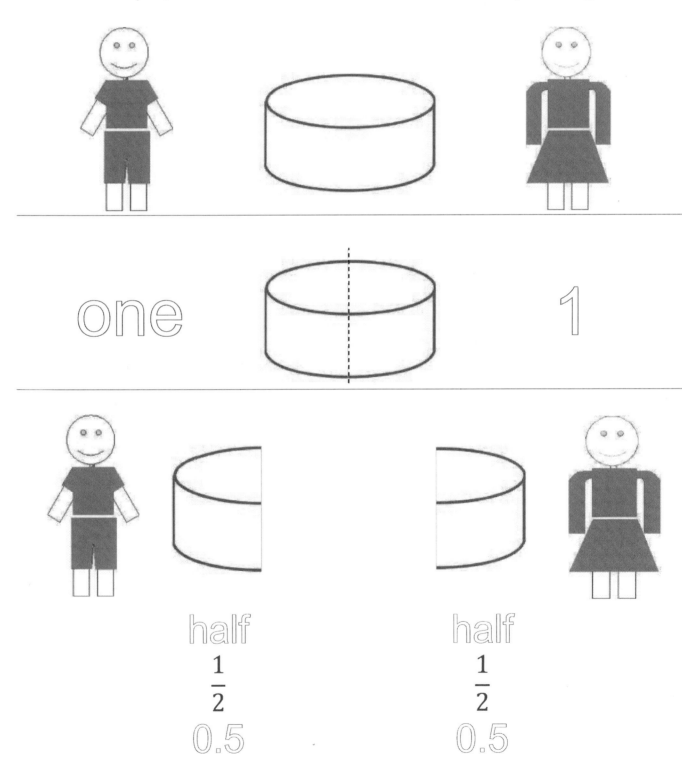

Also, if the same **two** children share **the same** whole **cake**, they can get **two-quarters** each. **Quarter** means **half of a half**.

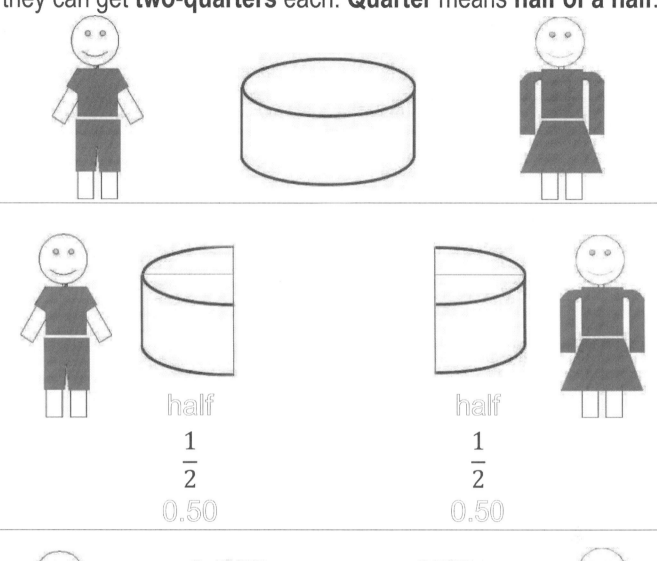

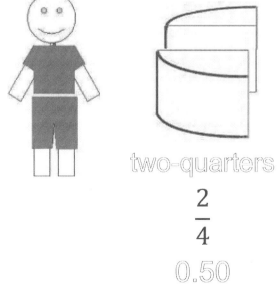

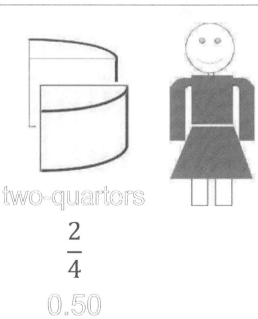

So, you can divide one whole cake into two halves (each child has a half) or into four quarters (every kid gets two-quarters).

Therefore, **half** is the same as **two-quarters**; both equal to **0.50**!

$$\frac{1}{2} = \frac{2}{4} = 0.50 \quad \text{or} \quad \square = \square .$$

Equivalent fractions are fractions with the **same value** even though their **numerators** and **denominators** may be **different**.

For example:

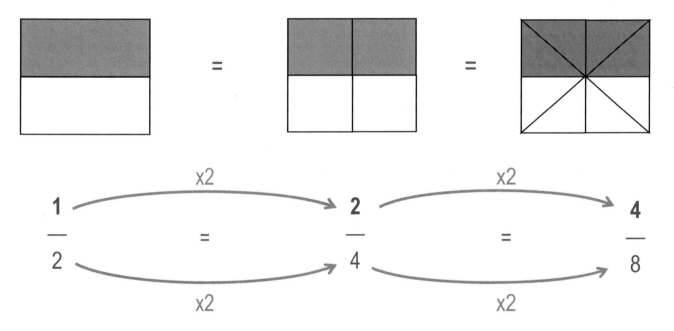

That is, if you **multiply** (or **divide**) both the numerator and the denominator of a fraction by the same non-zero number, **the value** of that fraction **always stays the same**!
The fraction only changes into a different equivalent fraction.

This is because multiplying the top and the bottom of a fraction by the same non-zero number is the same as multiplying that fraction by one!

Fifths of 5

Sharing *equally* for **5** people. Divided by 5. Five equal parts…

÷**5**	×$\frac{1}{5}$	×$^1/_5$

Use your *imagination* how to colour, **shade** and trace!

5 five

1 1 1 1 1

one one one one one

whole whole whole whole whole

Fifths of 1

Sharing *equally* for **5** people. Divided by 5. Five equal parts…

÷5	×$\frac{1}{5}$	×$^1/_5$

Use your imagination how to colour, **shade** and trace.

1

		$\frac{1}{5}$	0.2	fifth
		$\frac{1}{5}$	0.2	fifth
		$\frac{1}{5}$	0.2	fifth
		$\frac{1}{5}$	0.2	fifth
		$\frac{1}{5}$	0.2	fifth

one

Fifths of 2

Sharing *equally* for **5** people. Divided by 5. Five equal parts…

| ÷5 | ×$\frac{1}{5}$ | ×$1/5$ |

Use your *imagination* how to colour, **shade** and trace!

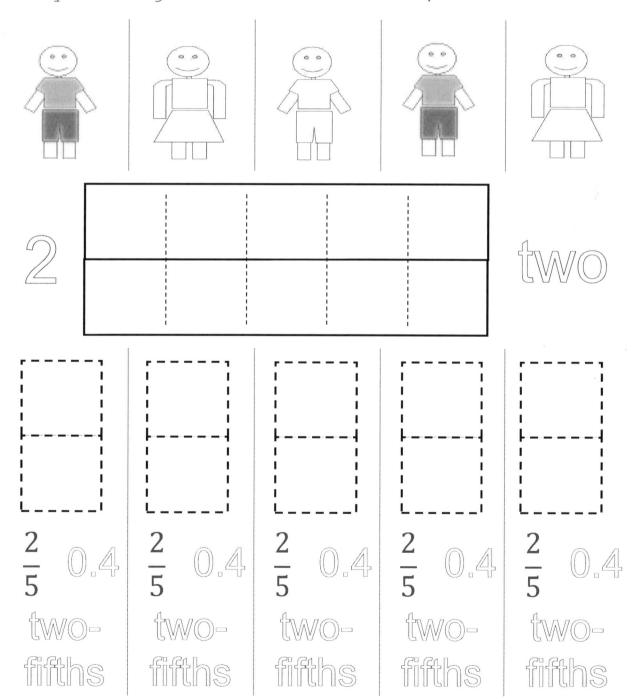

Fifths of 3

Sharing *equally* for **5** people. Divided by 5. Five equal parts...

÷5	×$\frac{1}{5}$	×$^1/_5$

Use your *imagination* how to colour, **shade** and trace!

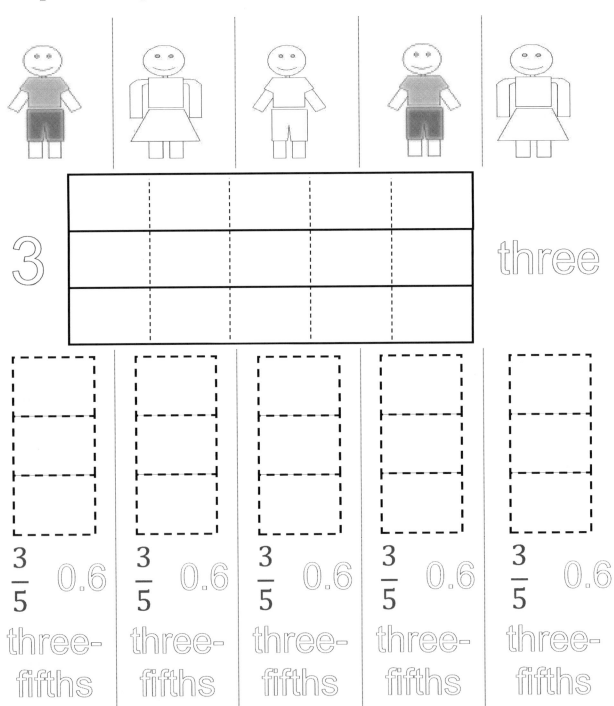

Fifths of 4

Sharing *equally* for **5** people. Divided by 5. Five equal parts...

| ÷5 | ×$\frac{1}{5}$ | ×$1/5$ |

Use your imagination how to colour, **shade** and trace.

four   4

$\frac{4}{5}$ $\frac{4}{5}$ $\frac{4}{5}$ $\frac{4}{5}$ $\frac{4}{5}$

0.8   0.8   0.8   0.8   0.8

four-fifths   four-fifths   four-fifths   four-fifths   four-fifths

Sixths of 6

Sharing *equally* for **6** people. Divided by 6. Six equal parts…

÷6	×$\frac{1}{6}$	×$^1/_6$

Use your imagination how to colour, **shade** and trace.

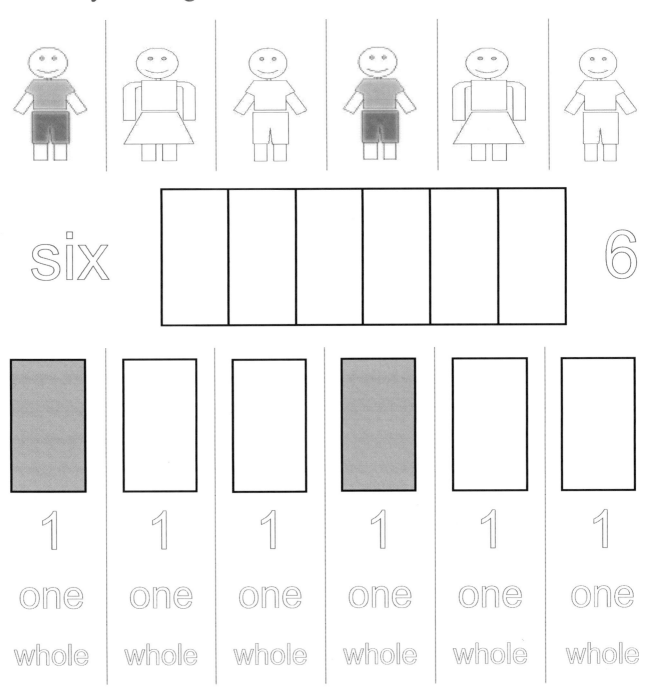

Sixths of 1

Sharing *equally* for **6** people. Divided by 6. Six equal parts...

÷6	×$\frac{1}{6}$	×$1/6$

Use your imagination how to colour, **shade** and trace.

1

$\frac{1}{6}$ 0.166 sixth

$\frac{1}{6}$ 0.166 sixth

$\frac{1}{6}$ 0.166 sixth

$\frac{1}{6}$ 0.166 sixth

$\frac{1}{6}$ 0.166 sixth

$\frac{1}{6}$ 0.166 sixth

one

Sixths of 2

Sharing *equally* for **6** people. Divided by 6. Six equal parts...

÷6	×$\frac{1}{6}$	×$^1/_6$

Use your imagination how to colour, **shade** and trace.

2

$\frac{2}{6}$ 0.33   two-sixths

$\frac{2}{6}$ 0.33   two-sixths

$\frac{2}{6}$ 0.33   two-sixths

$\frac{2}{6}$ 0.33   two-sixths

$\frac{2}{6}$ 0.33   two-sixths

$\frac{2}{6}$ 0.33   two-sixths

two

Sixths of 2

Sharing *equally* for **6** people. Divided by 6. Six equal parts...

÷6	×$\frac{1}{6}$	×$1/6$

Use your imagination how to colour, **shade** and trace.

2

$\frac{1}{3}$ 0.33   third

$\frac{1}{3}$ 0.33   third

$\frac{1}{3}$ 0.33   third

$\frac{1}{3}$ 0.33   third

$\frac{1}{3}$ 0.33   third

$\frac{1}{3}$ 0.33   third

two

Sixths of 3

Sharing *equally* for **6** people. Divided by 6. Six equal parts...

÷6	×$\frac{1}{6}$	×$1/6$

Use your imagination how to colour, **shade** and trace.

3

$\frac{3}{6}$ 0.5   three-sixths

$\frac{3}{6}$ 0.5   three-sixths

$\frac{3}{6}$ 0.5   three-sixths

$\frac{3}{6}$ 0.5   three-sixths

$\frac{3}{6}$ 0.5   three-sixths

$\frac{3}{6}$ 0.5   three-sixths

three

Sixths of 3

Sharing *equally* for **6** people. Divided by 6. Six equal parts…

÷6	×$\frac{1}{6}$	×$1/6$

Use your imagination how to colour, **shade** and trace.

3

		$\frac{1}{2}$	0.5	half
		$\frac{1}{2}$	0.5	half
		$\frac{1}{2}$	0.5	half
		$\frac{1}{2}$	0.5	half
		$\frac{1}{2}$	0.5	half
		$\frac{1}{2}$	0.5	half

three

Sixths of 4

Sharing *equally* for **6** people. Divided by 6. Six equal parts...

÷6	×$\frac{1}{6}$	×$^1/_6$

Use your imagination how to colour, **shade** and trace.

4

$\frac{4}{6}$ 0.66   four-sixths

$\frac{4}{6}$ 0.66   four-sixths

$\frac{4}{6}$ 0.66   four-sixths

$\frac{4}{6}$ 0.66   four-sixths

$\frac{4}{6}$ 0.66   four-sixths

$\frac{4}{6}$ 0.66   four-sixths

four

Sixths of 4

Sharing *equally* for **6** people. Divided by 6. Six equal parts…

÷6	×$\frac{1}{6}$	×$1/6$

Use your imagination how to colour, **shade** and trace.

4

	$\frac{2}{3}$	0.66	two-thirds
	$\frac{2}{3}$	0.66	two-thirds
	$\frac{2}{3}$	0.66	two-thirds
	$\frac{2}{3}$	0.66	two-thirds
	$\frac{2}{3}$	0.66	two-thirds
	$\frac{2}{3}$	0.66	two-thirds

four

Sixths of 5

Sharing *equally* for **6** people. Divided by 6. Six equal parts...

÷6	×$\frac{1}{6}$	×$^1/_6$

Use your imagination how to colour, **shade** and trace.

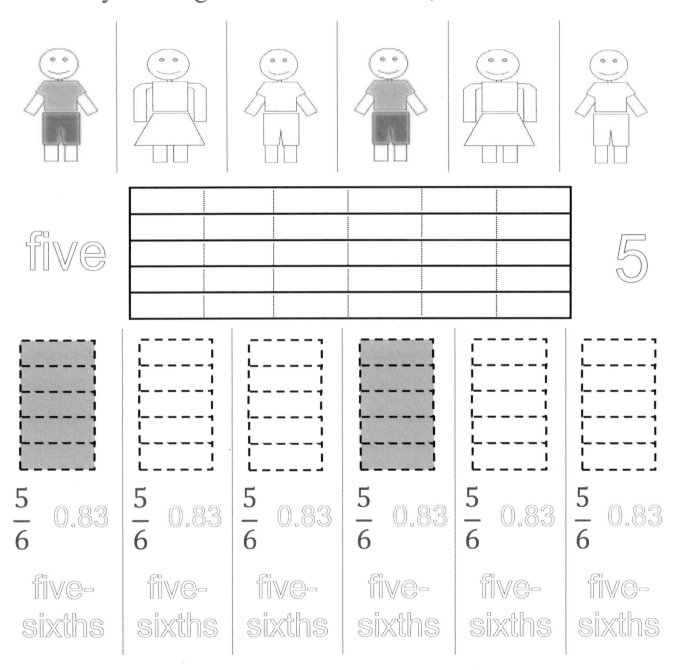

$\frac{5}{6}$ 0.83 | $\frac{5}{6}$ 0.83 | $\frac{5}{6}$ 0.83 | $\frac{5}{6}$ 0.83 | $\frac{5}{6}$ 0.83 | $\frac{5}{6}$ 0.83

five-sixths | five-sixths | five-sixths | five-sixths | five-sixths | five-sixths

Eighths of 8

Colour and trace the following **shape** for **8** friends sharing **8** shapes.

8			1	1.00	one whole
			1	1.00	one whole
			1	1.00	one whole
			1	1.00	one whole
			1	1.00	one whole
			1	1.00	one whole
			1	1.00	one whole
			1	1.00	one whole
eight					

Eighths of 2

Colour and trace the following **shape** for **8** friends sharing **2** shapes.

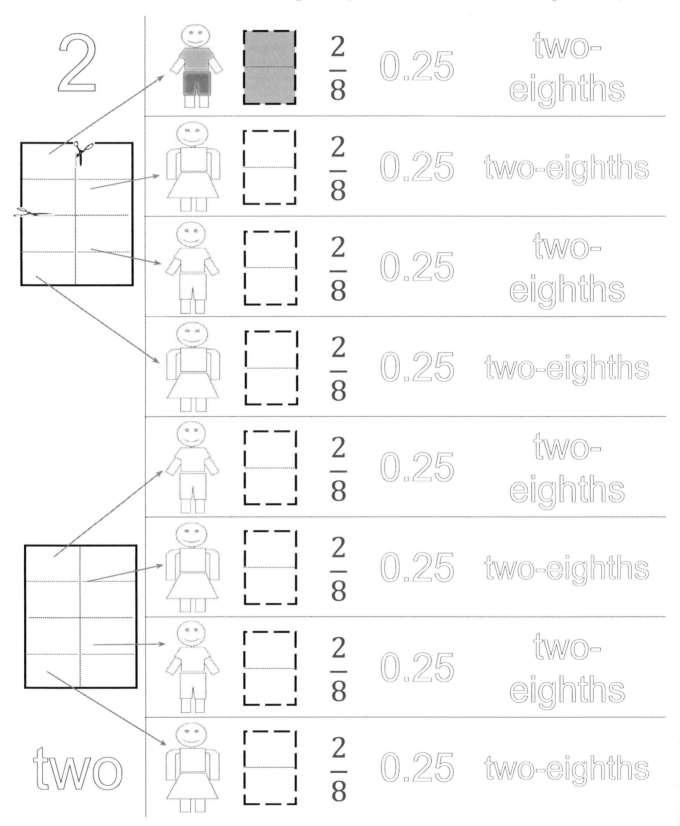

Eighths of 2

Colour and trace the following **shape** for **8** friends sharing **2** shapes.

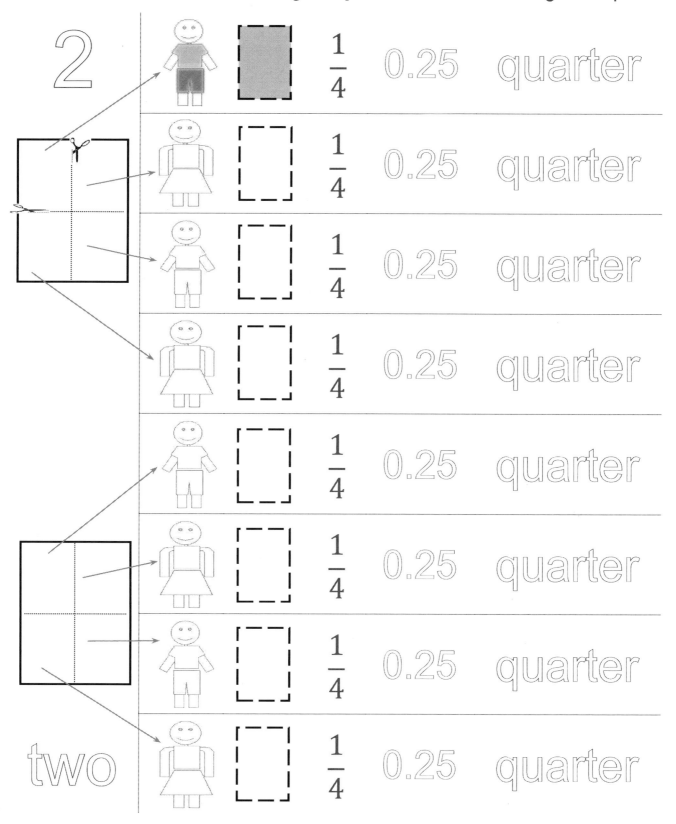

Eighths of 4

Colour and trace the following **shape** for **8** friends sharing **4** shapes.

4			$\frac{4}{8}$	0.5	four-eighths
			$\frac{4}{8}$	0.5	four-eighths
			$\frac{4}{8}$	0.5	four-eighths
			$\frac{4}{8}$	0.5	four-eighths
			$\frac{4}{8}$	0.5	four-eighths
			$\frac{4}{8}$	0.5	four-eighths
			$\frac{4}{8}$	0.5	four-eighths
four			$\frac{4}{8}$	0.5	four-eighths

Eighths of 4

Colour and trace the following **shape** for **8** friends sharing **4** shapes.

4

$\frac{2}{4}$ 0.5 half

$\frac{2}{4}$ 0.5 half

$\frac{2}{4}$ 0.5 half

$\frac{2}{4}$ 0.5 half

$\frac{2}{4}$ 0.5 half

$\frac{2}{4}$ 0.5 half

$\frac{2}{4}$ 0.5 half

four $\frac{2}{4}$ 0.5 half

Eighths of 6

Colour and trace the following **shape** for **8** friends sharing **6** shapes.

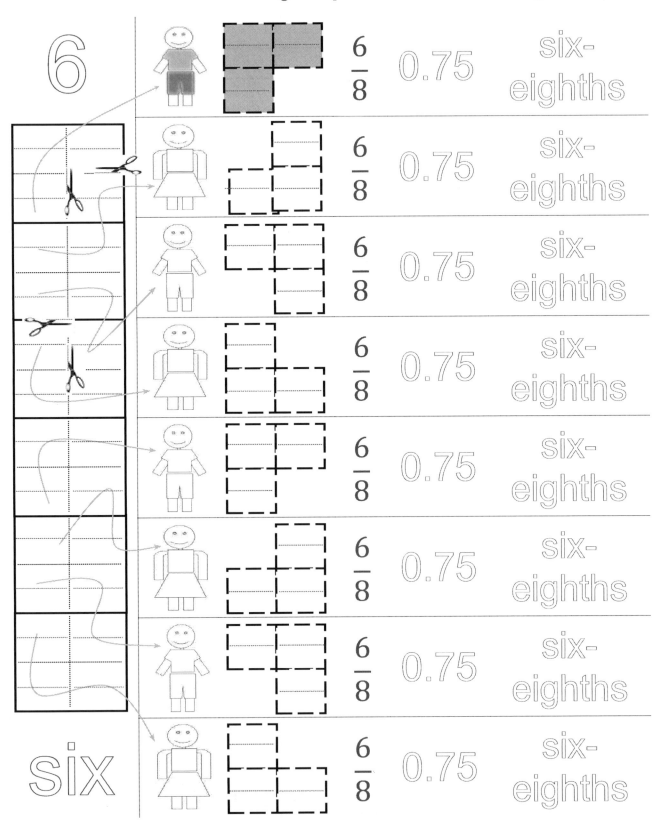

Eighths of 6

Colour and trace the following **shape** for **8** friends sharing **6** shapes.

		$\frac{3}{4}$	0.75	three-quarters
		$\frac{3}{4}$	0.75	three-quarters
		$\frac{3}{4}$	0.75	three-quarters
		$\frac{3}{4}$	0.75	three-quarters
		$\frac{3}{4}$	0.75	three-quarters
		$\frac{3}{4}$	0.75	three-quarters
		$\frac{3}{4}$	0.75	three-quarters
		$\frac{3}{4}$	0.75	three-quarters

six

Eighths of 1

Colour and trace the following shape for 8 friends sharing 1 shape.

eighth $\frac{1}{8}$ 0.125	$\frac{1}{8}$ eighth 0.125
$\frac{1}{8}$ 0.125 eighth	0.125 $\frac{1}{8}$ eighth
$\frac{1}{8}$ eighth 0.125	eighth $\frac{1}{8}$ 0.125
0.125 $\frac{1}{8}$ eighth	$\frac{1}{8}$ 0.125 eighth

one

Eighths of 3
Colour and trace the following **shape** for **8** friends sharing **3** shapes.

$\frac{3}{8}$	0.375	three-eighths
$\frac{3}{8}$	0.375	three-eighths
$\frac{3}{8}$	0.375	three-eighths
$\frac{3}{8}$	0.375	three-eighths
$\frac{3}{8}$	0.375	three-eighths
$\frac{3}{8}$	0.375	three-eighths
$\frac{3}{8}$	0.375	three-eighths
$\frac{3}{8}$	0.375	three-eighths

three

Eighths of 5

Colour and trace the following shape for 8 friends sharing 5 shapes.

		$\frac{5}{8}$	0.625	five-eighths
		$\frac{5}{8}$	0.625	five-eighths
		$\frac{5}{8}$	0.625	five-eighths
		$\frac{5}{8}$	0.625	five-eighths
		$\frac{5}{8}$	0.625	five-eighths
		$\frac{5}{8}$	0.625	five-eighths
		$\frac{5}{8}$	0.625	five-eighths
		$\frac{5}{8}$	0.625	five-eighths

five

Eighths of 7

Colour and trace the following **shape** for **8** friends sharing **7** shapes.

			$\frac{7}{8}$	0.875	seven-eighths
			$\frac{7}{8}$	0.875	seven-eighths
			$\frac{7}{8}$	0.875	seven-eighths
			$\frac{7}{8}$	0.875	seven-eighths
			$\frac{7}{8}$	0.875	seven-eighths
			$\frac{7}{8}$	0.875	seven-eighths
			$\frac{7}{8}$	0.875	seven-eighths
			$\frac{7}{8}$	0.875	seven-eighths

seven

Quiz 1

> Find the **odd one** out?
Which shape is **not** a proper **fraction** (*tick*)?

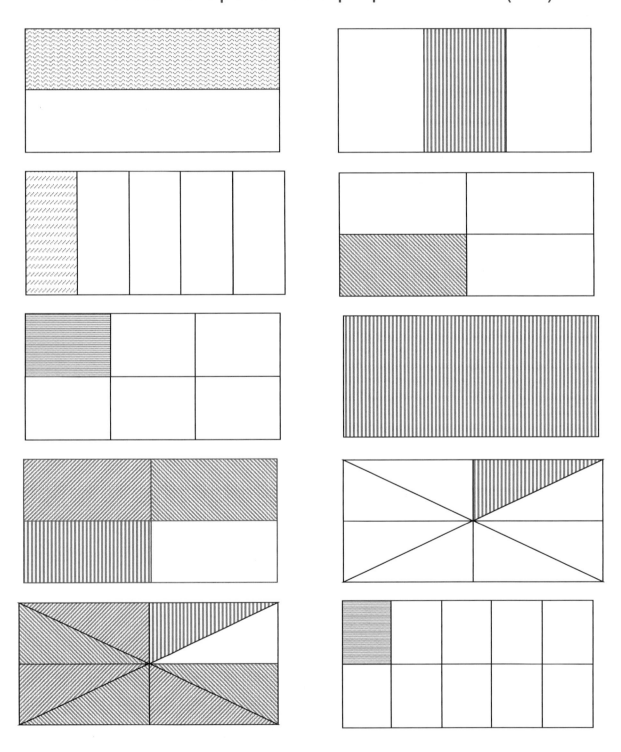

Ninths of 9

Sharing *equally* for **9** people. Divided by 9. Nine equal parts…

÷9	×$\frac{1}{9}$	×$^1/_9$

Use your imagination how to colour, **shade** and trace!

9

	1	1.00	one whole
	1	1.00	one whole
	1	1.00	one whole
	1	1.00	one whole
	1	1.00	one whole
	1	1.00	one whole
	1	1.00	one whole
	1	1.00	one whole
	1	1.00	one whole

nine

Ninths of 1

Sharing *equally* for **9** people. Divided by 9. Nine equal parts...

÷9	×$\frac{1}{9}$	×$^1/_9$

Use your imagination how to colour, **shade** and trace!

1

$\frac{1}{9}$ 0.111 ninth

$\frac{1}{9}$ 0.111 ninth

$\frac{1}{9}$ 0.111 ninth

$\frac{1}{9}$ 0.111 ninth

$\frac{1}{9}$ 0.111 ninth

$\frac{1}{9}$ 0.111 ninth

$\frac{1}{9}$ 0.111 ninth

$\frac{1}{9}$ 0.111 ninth

$\frac{1}{9}$ 0.111 ninth

one

Ninths of 2

Sharing *equally* for **9** people. Divided by 9. Nine equal parts...

÷9	×$\frac{1}{9}$	×$^1/_9$

Use your imagination how to colour, **shade** and trace!

2

$\frac{2}{9}$ 0.222 two-ninths

$\frac{2}{9}$ 0.222 two-ninths

$\frac{2}{9}$ 0.222 two-ninths

$\frac{2}{9}$ 0.222 two-ninths

$\frac{2}{9}$ 0.222 two-ninths

$\frac{2}{9}$ 0.222 two-ninths

$\frac{2}{9}$ 0.222 two-ninths

$\frac{2}{9}$ 0.222 two-ninths

$\frac{2}{9}$ 0.222 two-ninths

two

Ninths of 3

Sharing *equally* for **9** people. Divided by 9. Nine equal parts…

÷9	×$\frac{1}{9}$	×$1/9$

Use your imagination how to colour, **shade** and trace!

3

$\frac{3}{9}$ 0.333   three-ninths

$\frac{3}{9}$ 0.333   three-ninths

$\frac{3}{9}$ 0.333   three-ninths

$\frac{3}{9}$ 0.333   three-ninths

$\frac{3}{9}$ 0.333   three-ninths

$\frac{3}{9}$ 0.333   three-ninths

$\frac{3}{9}$ 0.333   three-ninths

$\frac{3}{9}$ 0.333   three-ninths

$\frac{3}{9}$ 0.333   three-ninths

three

Ninths of 3

Sharing *equally* for **9** people. Divided by 9. Nine equal parts…

÷9	×$\frac{1}{9}$	×$^1/_9$

Use your imagination how to colour, **shade** and trace!

3

		$\frac{1}{3}$	0.333	third
		$\frac{1}{3}$	0.333	third
		$\frac{1}{3}$	0.333	third
		$\frac{1}{3}$	0.333	third
		$\frac{1}{3}$	0.333	third
		$\frac{1}{3}$	0.333	third
		$\frac{1}{3}$	0.333	third
		$\frac{1}{3}$	0.333	third
		$\frac{1}{3}$	0.333	third

three

Ninths of 4

Sharing *equally* for **9** people. Divided by 9. Nine equal parts...

÷9	×$\frac{1}{9}$	×$1/9$

Use your imagination how to colour, **shade** and trace!

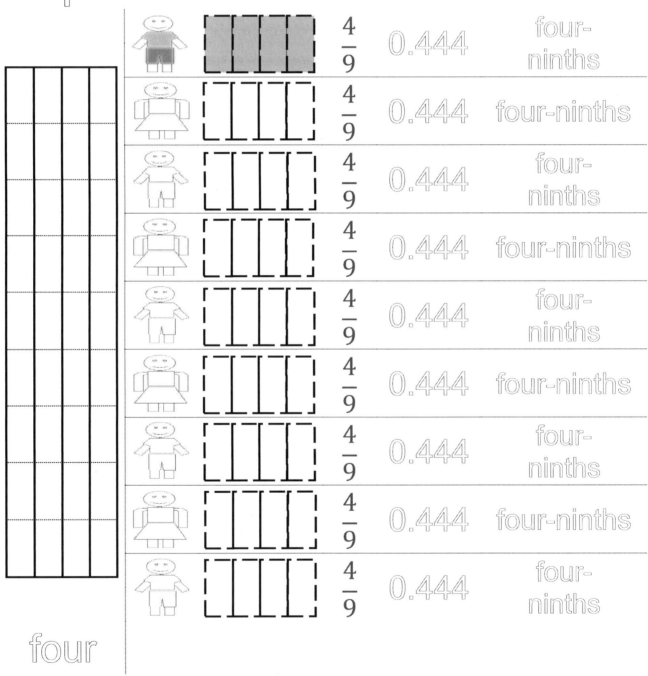

Ninths of 5

Sharing *equally* for **9** people. Divided by 9. Nine equal parts...

÷9	×$\frac{1}{9}$	×$^1/_9$

Use your imagination how to colour, **shade** and trace!

5

$\frac{5}{9}$ 0.555   five-ninths

$\frac{5}{9}$ 0.555   five-ninths

$\frac{5}{9}$ 0.555   five-ninths

$\frac{5}{9}$ 0.555   five-ninths

$\frac{5}{9}$ 0.555   five-ninths

$\frac{5}{9}$ 0.555   five-ninths

$\frac{5}{9}$ 0.555   five-ninths

$\frac{5}{9}$ 0.555   five-ninths

$\frac{5}{9}$ 0.555   five-ninths

five

Ninths of 6

Sharing *equally* for **9** people. Divided by 9. Nine equal parts…

÷9	×$\frac{1}{9}$	×$^1/_9$

Use your imagination how to colour, **shade** and trace.

6

$\frac{6}{9}$ 0.666 six-ninths

$\frac{6}{9}$ 0.666 six-ninths

$\frac{6}{9}$ 0.666 six-ninths

$\frac{6}{9}$ 0.666 six-ninths

$\frac{6}{9}$ 0.666 six-ninths

$\frac{6}{9}$ 0.666 six-ninths

$\frac{6}{9}$ 0.666 six-ninths

$\frac{6}{9}$ 0.666 six-ninths

$\frac{6}{9}$ 0.666 six-ninths

six

Ninths of 6

Sharing *equally* for **9** people. Divided by 9. Nine equal parts...

÷9	×$\frac{1}{9}$	×$^1/_9$

Use your imagination how to colour, **shade** and trace!

6

	$\frac{2}{3}$	0.666	two-thirds
	$\frac{2}{3}$	0.666	two-thirds
	$\frac{2}{3}$	0.666	two-thirds
	$\frac{2}{3}$	0.666	two-thirds
	$\frac{2}{3}$	0.666	two-thirds
	$\frac{2}{3}$	0.666	two-thirds
	$\frac{2}{3}$	0.666	two-thirds
	$\frac{2}{3}$	0.666	two-thirds
	$\frac{2}{3}$	0.666	two-thirds

six

Ninths of 7

Sharing *equally* for **9** people. Divided by 9. Nine equal parts...

÷9	×$\frac{1}{9}$	×$^1/_9$

Use your imagination how to colour, **shade** and trace!

7

$\frac{7}{9}$ 0.777 seven-ninths

$\frac{7}{9}$ 0.777 seven-ninths

$\frac{7}{9}$ 0.777 seven-ninths

$\frac{7}{9}$ 0.777 seven-ninths

$\frac{7}{9}$ 0.777 seven-ninths

$\frac{7}{9}$ 0.777 seven-ninths

$\frac{7}{9}$ 0.777 seven-ninths

$\frac{7}{9}$ 0.777 seven-ninths

$\frac{7}{9}$ 0.777 seven-ninths

seven

Ninths of 8

Sharing *equally* for **9** people. Divided by 9. Nine equal parts...

÷9	×$\frac{1}{9}$	×$^1/_9$

Use your imagination how to colour, **shade** and trace!

8

	$\frac{8}{9}$	0.888	eight-ninths
	$\frac{8}{9}$	0.888	eight-ninths
	$\frac{8}{9}$	0.888	eight-ninths
	$\frac{8}{9}$	0.888	eight-ninths
	$\frac{8}{9}$	0.888	eight-ninths
	$\frac{8}{9}$	0.888	eight-ninths
	$\frac{8}{9}$	0.888	eight-ninths
	$\frac{8}{9}$	0.888	eight-ninths
	$\frac{8}{9}$	0.888	eight-ninths

eight

Tenths of 10

Sharing *equally* for **10** people. Divided by 10. Ten equal parts…

| ÷10 | ×$\frac{1}{10}$ | ×$^1/_{10}$ |

Use your imagination how to colour, **shade** and trace!

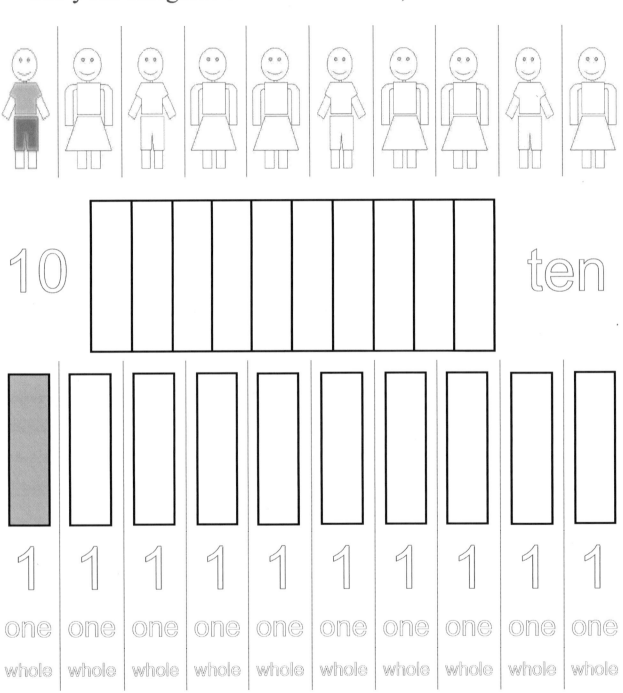

Tenths of 1

Sharing *equally* for **10** people. Divided by 10. Ten equal parts...

÷10	× $\frac{1}{10}$	× $^1/_{10}$

Use your imagination how to colour, **shade** and trace!

1

		$\frac{1}{10}$	0.10	tenth
		$\frac{1}{10}$	0.10	tenth
		$\frac{1}{10}$	0.10	tenth
		$\frac{1}{10}$	0.10	tenth
		$\frac{1}{10}$	0.10	tenth
		$\frac{1}{10}$	0.10	tenth
		$\frac{1}{10}$	0.10	tenth
		$\frac{1}{10}$	0.10	tenth
		$\frac{1}{10}$	0.10	tenth
		$\frac{1}{10}$	0.10	tenth

one

Tenths of 2

Sharing *equally* for **10** people. Divided by 10. Ten equal parts...

÷10	× $\frac{1}{10}$	× $^1/_{10}$

Use your imagination how to colour, **shade** and trace!

2

		$\frac{2}{10}$	0.20	two-tenths
		$\frac{2}{10}$	0.20	two-tenths
		$\frac{2}{10}$	0.20	two-tenths
		$\frac{2}{10}$	0.20	two-tenths
		$\frac{2}{10}$	0.20	two-tenths
		$\frac{2}{10}$	0.20	two-tenths
		$\frac{2}{10}$	0.20	two-tenths
		$\frac{2}{10}$	0.20	two-tenths
		$\frac{2}{10}$	0.20	two-tenths
		$\frac{2}{10}$	0.20	two-tenths

two

Tenths of 2

Sharing *equally* for **10** people. Divided by 10. Ten equal parts...

÷10	×$\frac{1}{10}$	×$^1/_{10}$

Use your imagination how to colour, **shade** and trace!

2

		$\frac{1}{5}$	0.20	fifth
		$\frac{1}{5}$	0.20	fifth
		$\frac{1}{5}$	0.20	fifth
		$\frac{1}{5}$	0.20	fifth
		$\frac{1}{5}$	0.20	fifth
		$\frac{1}{5}$	0.20	fifth
		$\frac{1}{5}$	0.20	fifth
		$\frac{1}{5}$	0.20	fifth
		$\frac{1}{5}$	0.20	fifth
		$\frac{1}{5}$	0.20	fifth

two

Tenths of 4

Sharing *equally* for **10** people. Divided by 10. Ten equal parts...

÷10	×$\frac{1}{10}$	×$^1/_{10}$

Use your imagination how to colour, **shade** and trace...

4

$\frac{4}{10}$ 0.40   four-tenths

$\frac{4}{10}$ 0.40   four-tenths

$\frac{4}{10}$ 0.40   four-tenths

$\frac{4}{10}$ 0.40   four-tenths

$\frac{4}{10}$ 0.40   four-tenths

$\frac{4}{10}$ 0.40   four-tenths

$\frac{4}{10}$ 0.40   four-tenths

$\frac{4}{10}$ 0.40   four-tenths

$\frac{4}{10}$ 0.40   four-tenths

$\frac{4}{10}$ 0.40   four-tenths

four

Tenths of 4

Sharing *equally* for **10** people. Divided by 10. Ten equal parts...

÷10	×$\frac{1}{10}$	×$^1/_{10}$

Use your imagination how to colour, **shade** and trace!

	$\frac{2}{5}$	0.40	two-fifths
	$\frac{2}{5}$	0.40	two-fifths
	$\frac{2}{5}$	0.40	two-fifths
	$\frac{2}{5}$	0.40	two-fifths
	$\frac{2}{5}$	0.40	two-fifths
	$\frac{2}{5}$	0.40	two-fifths
	$\frac{2}{5}$	0.40	two-fifths
	$\frac{2}{5}$	0.40	two-fifths
	$\frac{2}{5}$	0.40	two-fifths
	$\frac{2}{5}$	0.40	two-fifths

4

four

Tenths of 5

Sharing *equally* for **10** people. Divided by 10. Ten equal parts...

÷10	× $\frac{1}{10}$	×$^1/_{10}$

Use your imagination how to colour, **shade** and trace!

		$\frac{5}{10}$	0.50	five-tenths
		$\frac{5}{10}$	0.50	five-tenths
		$\frac{5}{10}$	0.50	five-tenths
		$\frac{5}{10}$	0.50	five-tenths
		$\frac{5}{10}$	0.50	five-tenths
		$\frac{5}{10}$	0.50	five-tenths
		$\frac{5}{10}$	0.50	five-tenths
		$\frac{5}{10}$	0.50	five-tenths
		$\frac{5}{10}$	0.50	five-tenths
		$\frac{5}{10}$	0.50	five-tenths

five

Tenths of 5

Sharing *equally* for **10** people. Divided by 10. Ten equal parts…

÷10	×$\frac{1}{10}$	×$^1/_{10}$

Use your imagination how to colour, **shade** and trace!

		$\frac{1}{2}$	0.50	half
		$\frac{1}{2}$	0.50	half
		$\frac{1}{2}$	0.50	half
		$\frac{1}{2}$	0.50	half
		$\frac{1}{2}$	0.50	half
		$\frac{1}{2}$	0.50	half
		$\frac{1}{2}$	0.50	half
		$\frac{1}{2}$	0.50	half
		$\frac{1}{2}$	0.50	half
		$\frac{1}{2}$	0.50	half

5

five

Tenths of 6

Sharing *equally* for **10** people. Divided by 10. Ten equal parts…

÷10	×$\frac{1}{10}$	×$^{1}/_{10}$

Use your imagination how to colour, **shade** and trace!

6

$\frac{6}{10}$ 0.60   six-tenths

$\frac{6}{10}$ 0.60   six-tenths

$\frac{6}{10}$ 0.60   six-tenths

$\frac{6}{10}$ 0.60   six-tenths

$\frac{6}{10}$ 0.60   six-tenths

$\frac{6}{10}$ 0.60   six-tenths

$\frac{6}{10}$ 0.60   six-tenths

$\frac{6}{10}$ 0.60   six-tenths

$\frac{6}{10}$ 0.60   six-tenths

$\frac{6}{10}$ 0.60   six-tenths

six

Tenths of 6

Sharing *equally* for **10** people. Divided by 10. Ten equal parts...

÷10	× $\frac{1}{10}$	× $1/10$

Use your imagination how to colour, **shade** and trace!

6

		$\frac{3}{5}$	0.60	three-fifths
		$\frac{3}{5}$	0.60	three-fifths
		$\frac{3}{5}$	0.60	three-fifths
		$\frac{3}{5}$	0.60	three-fifths
		$\frac{3}{5}$	0.60	three-fifths
		$\frac{3}{5}$	0.60	three-fifths
		$\frac{3}{5}$	0.60	three-fifths
		$\frac{3}{5}$	0.60	three-fifths
		$\frac{3}{5}$	0.60	three-fifths
		$\frac{3}{5}$	0.60	three-fifths

six

Tenths of 3

Sharing *equally* for **10** people. Divided by 10. Ten equal parts...

÷10	×$\frac{1}{10}$	×$^1/_{10}$

Use your imagination how to colour, **shade** and trace!

3

	$\frac{3}{10}$	0.30	three-tenths
	$\frac{3}{10}$	0.30	three-tenths
	$\frac{3}{10}$	0.30	three-tenths
	$\frac{3}{10}$	0.30	three-tenths
	$\frac{3}{10}$	0.30	three-tenths
	$\frac{3}{10}$	0.30	three-tenths
	$\frac{3}{10}$	0.30	three-tenths
	$\frac{3}{10}$	0.30	three-tenths
	$\frac{3}{10}$	0.30	three-tenths
	$\frac{3}{10}$	0.3	three-tenths

three

Tenths of 7

Sharing *equally* for **10** people. Divided by 10. Ten equal parts…

÷10	×$\frac{1}{10}$	×$^1/_{10}$

Use your imagination how to colour, **shade** and trace!

7

$\frac{7}{10}$ 0.70 seven-tenths

$\frac{7}{10}$ 0.70 seven-tenths

$\frac{7}{10}$ 0.70 seven-tenths

$\frac{7}{10}$ 0.70 seven-tenths

$\frac{7}{10}$ 0.70 seven-tenths

$\frac{7}{10}$ 0.70 seven-tenths

$\frac{7}{10}$ 0.70 seven-tenths

$\frac{7}{10}$ 0.70 seven-tenths

$\frac{7}{10}$ 0.70 seven-tenths

$\frac{7}{10}$ 0.70 seven-tenths

seven

Tenths of 8

Sharing *equally* for **10** people. Divided by 10. Ten equal parts...

÷10	×$\frac{1}{10}$	×$^1/_{10}$

Use your imagination how to colour, **shade** and trace!

8

$\frac{8}{10}$ 0.80 eight-tenths

$\frac{8}{10}$ 0.80 eight-tenths

$\frac{8}{10}$ 0.80 eight-tenths

$\frac{8}{10}$ 0.80 eight-tenths

$\frac{8}{10}$ 0.80 eight-tenths

$\frac{8}{10}$ 0.80 eight-tenths

$\frac{8}{10}$ 0.80 eight-tenths

$\frac{8}{10}$ 0.80 eight-tenths

$\frac{8}{10}$ 0.80 eight-tenths

$\frac{8}{10}$ 0.80 eight-tenths

eight

Tenths of 8

Sharing *equally* for **10** people. Divided by 10. Ten equal parts...

÷10	× $\frac{1}{10}$	× $1/10$

Use your imagination how to colour, **shade** and trace!

8

			$\frac{4}{5}$	0.80	four-fifths
			$\frac{4}{5}$	0.80	four-fifths
			$\frac{4}{5}$	0.80	four-fifths
			$\frac{4}{5}$	0.80	four-fifths
			$\frac{4}{5}$	0.80	four-fifths
			$\frac{4}{5}$	0.80	four-fifths
			$\frac{4}{5}$	0.80	four-fifths
			$\frac{4}{5}$	0.80	four-fifths
			$\frac{4}{5}$	0.80	four-fifths
			$\frac{4}{5}$	0.80	four-fifths

eight

Tenths of 9

Sharing *equally* for **10** people. Divided by 10. Ten equal parts...

÷10	×$\frac{1}{10}$	×$^1/_{10}$

Use your imagination how to colour, **shade** and trace!

9

$\frac{9}{10}$ 0.90   nine-tenths

$\frac{9}{10}$ 0.90   nine-tenths

$\frac{9}{10}$ 0.90   nine-tenths

$\frac{9}{10}$ 0.90   nine-tenths

$\frac{9}{10}$ 0.90   nine-tenths

$\frac{9}{10}$ 0.90   nine-tenths

$\frac{9}{10}$ 0.90   nine-tenths

$\frac{9}{10}$ 0.90   nine-tenths

$\frac{9}{10}$ 0.90   nine-tenths

$\frac{9}{10}$ 0.90   nine-tenths

nine

Quiz 2

◁ Find the **odd one** out!

Which of the following numbers is **not** a proper **fraction** (*circle*)?

$$\frac{1}{2} \qquad \frac{1}{3}$$

$$\frac{1}{5} \qquad \frac{1}{4}$$

$$\frac{1}{6} \qquad \frac{1}{9}$$

$$\frac{1}{7} \qquad \frac{3}{4} \qquad \frac{1}{8}$$

$$\frac{1}{10} \qquad \frac{1}{1} \qquad 1$$

Copyright © Eng S Jama
All rights reserved.

author.to/FractionsVisually | https://fractionsvisually.com

Thank you for buying my book and helping the author to keep on writing. ☺

I hope you've enjoyed reading UNDERSTANDING FRACTIONS VISUALLY COLOURING WORKBOOK.

If so, please, consider leaving a review on ***Amazon.com*** *at* amazon.com/review/create-review?&asin=**1723563986**.
A single line, short sentence, few phrases or just rating will do.

If not, please, send me your feedback, comments and corrections to: *eng-s-jama@fractionsvisually.com*.

Thanks.

--- *Series #1:* UNDERSTANDING FRACTIONS VISUALLY ---

Colouring **workbook**: mybook.to/WB1-Sh-v2   **Paperback**: mybook.to/B-1
Colour **paperback**: mybook.to/B1-C   Colour **ebook**: mybook.to/eB1-C
Workbook: mybook.to/WB-1   Colour **workbook**: mybook.to/WB1-C

--- *Series #2:* ADDING FRACTIONS VISUALLY ---

Paperback: mybook.to/B-2   Colour **paperback**: mybook.to/B2-C
Workbook: mybook.to/WB2   Colour **workbook**: mybook.to/WB2-C
Colouring workbook: mybook.to/WB2-Sh   **Colour ebook**: mybook.to/eB2-C

--- *Series #3:* ADDING FRACTIONS *STEP-BY-STEP* ---

Paperback: mybook.to/B-3   Colour **paperback**: mybook.to/B3-C
Workbook: mybook.to/WB3   Colour **workbook**: mybook.to/WB3-C

--- *Series #4:* UNDERSTAND, ADD & SUBTRACT FRACTIONS VISUALLY ---

Paperback: mybook.to/B-4   Colour **paperback**: mybook.to/B4-C

UNDERSTANDING FRACTIONS VISUALLY
COLOURING WORKBOOK

Ages 5 – 11

Alex   Ella   Ali   Asha

Primary Education

For Children Who Think Fractions Are No Fun

Nearly 5000 fraction **shapes**, fraction **names**, **decimal** fractions and images to **colour**, shade and trace.

Endless fun and visual activities to enjoy mastering basic maths fractions using shape and fraction association.

Fractions, equivalent fraction, decimal fractions and percentages.

Comparison of fractions families, illustrations, images, kids characters, quick quizzes and easy fractions vocabulary.

Have fun ☺

On Amazon Marketplaces:

mybook.to/WB1-Sh-v2

ENG S JAMA

author.to/FractionsVisually   amazon.co.uk/FractionsVisually

Made in the USA
Las Vegas, NV
16 October 2022

5742581 1R00059